I0816600

★★★★★
MLB TEAMS

Pittsburgh PIRATES

KENNY ABDO

Fly!
An Imprint of Abdo Zoom
abdobooks.com

abdobooks.com

Published by Abdo Zoom, a division of ABDO, P.O. Box 398166, Minneapolis, Minnesota 55439.

Printed in the United States of America, North Mankato, Minnesota.
102025
012026

Photo Credits: AP Images, Getty Images, Shutterstock
Production Contributors: Kenny Abdo, Jennie Forsberg, Grace Hansen
Design Contributors: Candice Keimig, Neil Klinepier

Library of Congress Control Number: 2025936809

Publisher's Cataloging-in-Publication Data

Names: Abdo, Kenny, author.
Title: Pittsburgh Pirates / by Kenny Abdo
Description: Minneapolis, Minnesota : Abdo Zoom, 2026 | Series: MLB teams | Includes online resources and index.
Identifiers: ISBN 9798384940296 (lib. bdg.) | ISBN 9798384941057 (ebook) | ISBN 9798384941439 (read-to-me ebook)
Subjects: LCSH: Pittsburgh Pirates (Baseball team)--Juvenile literature. | Baseball teams--Juvenile literature. | Professional sports--Juvenile literature. | Sports franchises--Juvenile literature. | Major League Baseball (Organization)--Juvenile literature.
Classification: DDC 796.357--dc23

Table of CONTENTS

PIRATES

With a handful of World Series titles and a lineup filled with famous base stealers, the Pittsburgh Pirates have sailed through baseball history for more than 140 years!

With gold on their minds and bats in their hands, the Pirates rule the diamond and remain a treasure to the city of Pittsburgh!

BATTER UP!

The Pittsburgh Pirates entered the **National League (NL)** in 1887. In 1902, the team had an epic season with 103 wins and only 36 losses. It was the league's best **record** that year!

In 1909, the Pirates won their first World Series. Led by star shortstop Honus Wagner, the team earned a win over the Tigers.

That season, the Pirates also won 110 games, a **franchise record** that still stands today.

The Pirates won the World Series again in 1925. They came back from being down 3–1 to beat the Washington Senators 4–3. The team returned to the World Series in 1927 but lost to a strong Yankees lineup.

GRAND SLAMS

The Pirates were strong in the 1950s and '60s. Star outfielder Roberto Clemente helped lead the way to the Fall Classic. In 1960, amazed fans watched as Bill Mazeroski's Game 7 **walk-off** home run sailed over the fence to win the World Series. It was one of the most dramatic home runs in Major League Baseball (MLB) history.

PIRATES
PIRATES
16
40

STARGELL
8

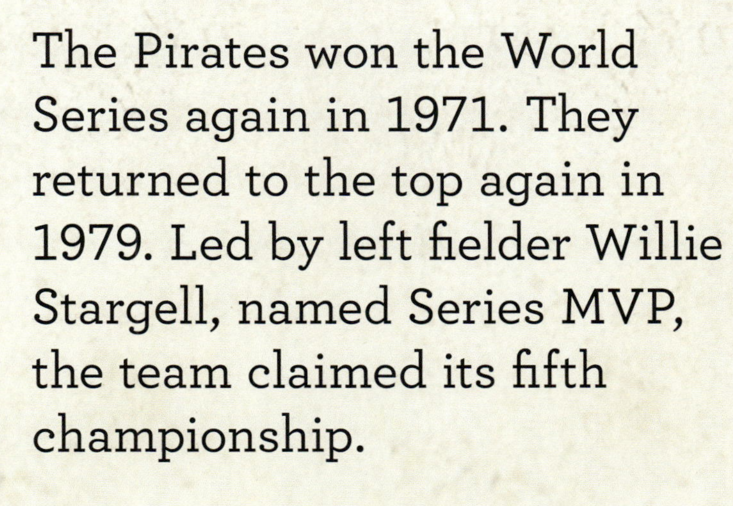

The Pirates won the World Series again in 1971. They returned to the top again in 1979. Led by left fielder Willie Stargell, named Series MVP, the team claimed its fifth championship.

The Pirates won three straight **division** titles from 1990 to 1992, with help from stars like Barry Bonds and Andy Van Slyke.

After that run, the team missed the playoffs for more than 20 years. Fans had to wait a long time for the next big chance.

In 2013, the Pirates finally returned to the **postseason**. Center fielder Andrew McCutchen led Pittsburgh to a 94-win season and an **NL wild-card** spot, the first of three in a row. Although they only advanced to the **Division** Series once, fans saw it as a sign that the Pirates could be a winning team. The rest of the decade was a struggle, but hopes still ran high.

22

Flow
SKENES
30

In 2022, Oneil Cruz recorded one of the hardest-hit balls in MLB history at 122.4 mph. He topped that in 2025 with a 122.9 mph home run. That same year, Paul Skenes made his second straight **All-Star** team. With rising stars and loyal fans, the Buccos look toward smoother sailing ahead.

HALL OF FAME

Honus Wagner was one of the best hitters and shortstops in baseball history. He helped the Pirates win the 1909 World Series and led the league in batting eight times. His baseball card is still one of the rarest and most valuable in the world. Wagner entered the Baseball Hall of Fame in 1936.

P

Roberto Clemente was a powerful hitter and a fast outfielder with a rocket arm. He helped the Pirates win the World Series in 1960 and again in 1971. Clemente won the **NL** MVP in 1966, earned 12 **Gold Gloves**, and took home four batting titles. He finished with exactly 3,000 hits. Clemente was named to the Hall of Fame in 1973.

P
PIRATES
8

Willie Stargell crushed 475 home runs as a Pirate. He won the **NL** MVP and shared the World Series MVP in 1979. That same year, Stargell helped the "We Are Family" Pirates win their fifth title. He played his entire 21-year career in Pittsburgh and entered the Hall of Fame in 1988.

GLOSSARY

All-Star – consisting of athletes chosen as the best at their positions from all teams in a league or region.

division – a number of teams grouped together in a sport for competitive purposes.

franchise – a sports organization, including the top-level team and all minor league affiliates.

Gold Glove Award – an annual award given to the best fielders at each position in both the American League (AL) and NL.

National League (NL) – one of two 15-team leagues that make up MLB.

postseason – the playoffs, including the wild-card round, divisional playoffs, league championship series, and World Series.

record – a team's season total of wins and losses; a top achievement by a team.

walk-off – any victory in which the home team scores the winning run in the bottom of the final inning.

wild-card – a place or a team chosen to fill a place in a competition after the regularly qualified players or teams have all been decided.

ONLINE RESOURCES

To learn more about the Pittsburgh Pirates, please visit abdobooklinks.com or scan this QR code. These links are routinely monitored and updated to provide the most current information available.

INDEX